# Stourbridge, Wollaston & Amblecote

BRITAIN IN OLD PHOTOGRAPHS

# STOURBRIDGE, WOLLASTON & AMBLECOTE

BOB CLARKE &
MICHAEL REUTER

SUTTON PUBLISHING LIMITED

Sutton Publishing Limited
Phoenix Mill · Thrupp · Stroud
Gloucestershire · GL5 2BU

First published 1997

**British Library Cataloguing in Publication Data**
A catalogue record for this book is available from the
British Library.

ISBN 0-7509-1457-2

Typeset in 10/12 Perpetua.
Typesetting and origination by
Sutton Publishing Limited.
Printed in Great Britain by
Ebenezer Baylis, Worcester.

# THE BLACK COUNTRY SOCIETY

This voluntary society, affiliated to the Civic Trust, was founded in 1967 as a reaction to the trend of the late 1950s and early 1960s to amalgamate everything into large units and in the Midlands to sweep away the area's industrial heritage in the process.

The general aim of the Society is to create interest in the past, present and future of the Black Country, and early on it campaigned for the establishment of an industrial museum. In 1975 the Black Country Museum was started by Dudley Borough Council on 26 acres of totally derelict land adjoining the grounds of Dudley Castle. This has developed into an award-winning museum which attracts over 250,000 visitors annually.

At the Black Country Museum there is a boat dock fully equipped to restore narrow boats of wood and iron and different boats can be seen on the dock throughout the year. From behind the Bottle and Glass Inn visitors can travel on a canal boat into Dudley Canal Tunnel, a memorable journey to see spectacular limestone caverns and the fascinating Castle Mill Basin.

There are over two-thousand members of the Black Country Society and all receive the quarterly magazine *The Blackcountryman*, of which over 119 issues have been published since its founding in 1967. In the whole collection there are some 1,700 authoritative articles on all aspects of the Black Country by historians, teachers, researchers, students, subject experts and ordinary folk with an extraordinary story to tell. The whole constitutes a unique resource about the area and is a mine of information for students and researchers who frequently refer to it. Many schools and libraries are subscribers. Three-thousand copies of the magazine are printed each quarter. It is non-commercial, and contributors do not receive payment for their articles.

*PO Box 71 · Kingswinford · West Midlands DY6 9YN*

# CONTENTS

The town clock, probably the best-known feature in Stourbridge town and certainly one of the most photographed. Erected in 1857 at the entrance of the old market hall and mounted on a cast-iron fluted pillar, it was constructed at the Stourbridge ironworks of John Bradley & Co. and designed by the works engineer, William Millward. Moves to resite the clock by Dudley Metropolitan Borough Council were roundly defeated by local opposition and, after refurbishment, the clock was returned to its original site.

# INTRODUCTION

The Borough of Stourbridge, which included Stambermill, Lye, Wollescote, Pedmore, Norton, Wollaston and, for a short time, part of Amblecote, ceased to exist over twenty-three years ago when local government in England and Wales was reorganized. The town and its immediate surroundings have, nevertheless, retained much of their own character, developed over the centuries as a North Worcestershire market town on the southern edge of the Black Country.

It was considered, in estate agents' jargon, 'a sought-after place' in which to live by many of the Black Country's leading industrialists from the early nineteenth century. And it still retains considerable appeal being on the very edge of the conurbation, close to the motorway network and adjoining the unspoilt countryside of North Worcestershire and South Staffordshire.

There has always been and doubtless will continue to be a lively debate as to whether Stourbridge is part of the Black Country. If you take the definition of the Black Country as being an area within a 5 mile radius of Dudley Top Church then the answer is 'yes' – just. But if you take the alternative view that the Black Country is the area under which there lay the 30 ft 'thick' – a seam of high-quality coal that fed the Industrial Revolution locally – then the answer is 'no', as much of Stourbridge lies on sandstone.

Whether Stourbridge is or is not part of the Black Country matters not. Its development as a trading centre grew with the Industrial Revolution, although before then it was the recognized centre for glassmaking following the arrival of European glassmakers fleeing from religious persecution on the Continent.

By the nineteenth century Stourbridge was well established as both a prosperous Worcestershire market town and an industrial area.

For centuries, Oldswinford (with a brief mention in the Domesday Book) remained the 'centre' of Stourbridge before industry and canal and rail transport in the late eighteenth and mid-nineteenth centuries respectively heralded the start of a new era.

The story of Stourbridge's growth, therefore, is similar in many ways to other Black Country towns; the difference is that it has that indefinable 'extra' of still retaining something of its early days as a market town.

It is said that Stourbridge and the surrounding areas which formed the municipal borough lost much of their heritage and individuality when the borough was forcibly amalgamated within the large (and some say impersonal) Dudley Metropolitan Borough. We leave the reader to make the final judgement on this point after seeing in the following pages examples of the Stourbridge of previous years and comparing them with the Stourbridge and district of today.

Every town of note had its 'comic' greetings cards; usually they were of a standard design with the town or area's name being printed as required. These are two examples of a number of such cards which were popular in Stourbridge during the interwar years.

# STOURBRIDGE

*Lower High Street, Stourbridge with a Dudley-bound tram heading down the hill at the turn of the twentieth century. To the right are boys presumably from King Edward VI Grammar School, while on the left a policeman is talking to a local trader.*

The market hall was opened in 1827, having cost £20,000 to construct. This is one of the earliest known drawings of the building which replaced the original town hall (or market hall) that had been demolished in 1773 when the town centre was expanded.

Looking up the High Street, *c.* 1910. Trams ran through Stourbridge for about twenty-five years and went up the narrow High Street to a terminus outside the public library at its junction with Hagley Road.

Until quite recently Coventry Street had a concentration of small shops. On the left is Marsh & Baxter's temporary shop, while not far away, on the right, was a clothes shop (identity unknown). The street was also well known for the number of butchers' shops – at one time there were no fewer than five.

Coventry Street, late 1920s. To the right is the Old Bank (London City & Midland Bank). Beyond the bank, on the right-hand side of Coventry Street, much of the property has been demolished while that on the left has remained largely untouched.

Nickolls & Perks off-licence was formerly known as the Board Inn and is believed to be one of the town's oldest surviving commercial buildings. A chapel for Dissenters had been built at the rear of an older building on the site in 1698 but was burnt down by rioters in 1715.

Two contrasting views. Above, a police officer is on point duty in the town centre where four main thoroughfares meet,, well before traffic lights were installed. The area where the policeman is standing is now pedestrianized. Below, a more leisurely scene. Numerous pedal cycles, a horse and cart and a tramcar form the only road traffic; the schoolboys in the foreground seem to be paying more attention to the photographer than the approaching tramcar!

King Edward VI Grammar School, late 1920s. This is the oldest school in the area, originally founded as a chantry school in 1430. Closed during the dissolution and reopened by command of King Edward VI in 1552, it had a long and illustrious history of academic excellence. It became a sixth-form college in 1976; thus, with a single stroke of a Whitehall pen, over 400 years of tradition was wiped out. The headmaster's house and senior master's house to the right of the tower were demolished to make way for the assembly hall, opened in 1931. To the left of the tower was the former school hall which then became the library, while on the extreme left was the staff room.

The staff of King Edward VI School, 1949. Front row, left to right: C.W.P. Aggleton, Miss J. Reid, Miss I.D. Druller, Miss D.M. Wicks, F. Carter (deputy headmaster), T.W. Watson (headmaster), H.G. Easterling, G.H.C. Burley, W.E. Dempsey, W.A. Kitson, S.J. Featherstone, R.F.C. Edwards. Centre row: J. McFarlane, F.M. Williams, I.W. Stray, E. Wright, W.R. Elliott, W. Parsons, H.H. Edwards, T. Crippen, G.I. Rollason, C.V. White. Back row: M.G. Lucy, F. Lawley, T.E.L. Chataway, J.J. Anderson, A.H. Nicholls, D.W. Waters, H.W. Shotton, M.T. Parker.

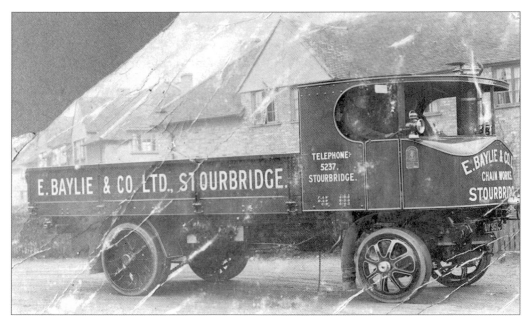

The steam-powered lorry (above) of the well-known chain-making concern of E. Baylie & Co. Ltd.
Although Stourbridge was only considered to be on the fringe of the Black Country, many traditional
Black Country industries thrived. This form of transport contrasted greatly with the petrol-engined solid-
tyred lorry (below).

Employees of Baylie's chain works proudly display their membership of the Chain Makers & Strikers Association trade union, the national headquarters of which were in the Institute Building, Lower High Street (formerly Lomey Town), Cradley Heath.

The Cross Keys Inn, New Street, 1925. Demolished to make way for the Crown shopping centre and market hall, New Street was home to a fascinating collection of old buildings almost all of which had been converted into commercial premises.

An old-established firm of auto engineers was Taylor's whose premises were in Victoria Street. Members of the Taylor family and staff demonstrate their prowess on penny-farthing and other vintage cycles.

There are few photographs of the founder of one of the earliest pioneers of motor-coach travel in the district – Samuel Johnson – whose 'Supreme' fleet always included the latest models. This photograph, taken in the early 1920s, includes 'Sammy' Johnson on the extreme right. The rest of the people pictured were members of the local fire brigade on their annual outing – presumably Mr Johnson was driving. Among them are George Banks, Joe Stell, George Whitehead, Percy Harper, Messrs Marley (brothers?), Tom Sidaway, Bill Weaver, Captain C. Walker, Harold Bingham, Joe Grant, Fred Griffin, Bert Marsh.

Although the simultaneous opening of the Stourbridge and Dudley canals in 1979 gave considerable impetus to trade – particularly the mining and ironworking industries – the arrival of the railway in 1852 linked an already prosperous town first with Worcester and Wolverhampton and then, as the network expanded, with the rest of the nation's towns and cities by the end of the nineteenth century. The first route to Stourbridge was the Oxford, Worcester and Wolverhampton (OW & W) railway; it soon became known as the 'Old Worse & Worse' on account of the number of accidents which occurred on it. In Amblecote there was a particularly serious one in which some people died when a coupling on a homeward-bound and overloaded day-excursion train snapped near Brettell Lane; several coaches ran backwards down towards Amblecote to be rammed by a following excursion train. In 1863 the OW & W was amalgamated with the Great Western Railway. In the same year the Stourbridge Railway between what then became the Junction station to Birmingham (Snow Hill) opened and in 1870 also became part of the GWR. At about the same time a branch line was opened to the town with a further extension down a steep incline to a goods yard and canal interchange basin in Amblecote. Although the canal basin and goods yard were eventually removed to make way for a large industrial estate, the Town station has remained despite the occasional threat in past years to its future and now adjoins a large bus station. This is thought to be a 'City' class 4–4–0 from about 1910. It is heading a Cardiff–Birmingham express past the signal box. It was an engine of the 'City' class which topped 100 mph on a scheduled run between London and Plymouth.

Junction station, *c.* 1951. By this time the traditional pristine condition of GWR stations had disappeared as can be seen from this platform surface. The *Prairie* tank engine appears to have finished duty and is returning to the Amblecote engine sheds, while on the left a Worcester express waits for the signal to leave.

Stourbridge Town station complete with its 'push and pull' – or 'Town Dodger' – single-coach train waiting at the platform ready for its 1-mile journey to the Junction station, *c.* 1930. The other line crossed Foster Street and went down a steep incline to the goods yard and canal interchange basin adjoining the gasworks. The whole of that land is now covered by the Mill Lane Industrial Estate – an area which many critics of today's ring road believe should have been used to keep the ring road further away from the town centre.

The first viaduct (above) across the Stour Valley was the then traditional timber-trestle style mounted on brick pillars on the valley floor. Later in the nineteenth century, at about the time the Great Western Railway absorbed the OW & W, the timber viaduct was replaced after a double-track brick-built viaduct was constructed alongside. Traces of the foundations of the original viaduct can still be seen. Below is an early photograph (from about 1890) of the new viaduct taken from farmland where the Penfields housing estate now stands.

The viaduct viewed from the Stambermill side, 1950s. In the background are factory premises behind which is waste land where a housing estate now stands. Also in the far background can be seen the mills which stood alongside the River Stour. At a maximum height of 98 feet above the valley floor, the viaduct's arches each have a span of 46 feet.

Above, the crew of this goods train had to jump for their lives when their locomotive left the rails just before it went on to the viaduct and slid down the embankment towards the river. Trucks piled on top of it, but its whereabouts can still be made out from the smoke and steam rising from the wreckage. Ironically, the word on one of the trucks can be clearly read as 'SHOCK'. Below, such was the nature of the incline from Stourbridge Town station to the Amblecote goods yard that goods wagons were carefully brought down a few at a time, particularly because in the early days not all the trucks had vacuum brakes operated from the engine. Occasionally trains used to run away with spectacular results when they hit the buffers near the goods station offices. On one occasion wreckage finished up on the pavement of Lower High Street.

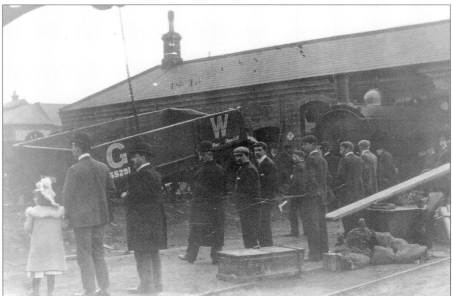

Judging by the type of 2–4–2 tank engine in the background – with its number plate between the words 'Great Western' – the top picture was probably taken in about 1920. Number plates were later mounted on cab sides. Below, a group of railway men and supervisors at the Amblecote 'shed' from about the same time. Behind them can be seen the water tank and the coaling area for the locomotives.

The GWR men of Stourbridge, proud of their first-aid expertise, and the men of Stourbridge Junction station (including those of Town station) display the trophies they had won in national and regional competitions (above). Trouble struck the Lower High Street goods station and surrounding property (right) when the River Stour burst its banks on 1/2 June 1924. After a deluge of 3.73 inches fell in twelve hours the whole vicinity came to a standstill with workmen salvaging barrels and drums which had been washed away. In the background is the footbridge across the goods yard.

Lower High Street, *c.* 1925. All the property in the foreground was demolished to make way for the ring road, but when this picture was taken the imposing façades retained much of their architectural interest. In the background is one of the town's gas holders (just 'over the border' in Amblecote). The buildings in front of the gasworks were part of the GWR goods yard and a railway track ran across the road into a local ironworks and foundry.

Lower High Street during the great flood of 1924. The area remained something of a flood risk for many years until the Upper Stour Valley Main Sewerage Board, who were responsible for the river, carried out improvements by dredging and improving the river's course.

The white-faced building, 23 Lower High Street, was bought by King Edward VI School and demolished for extensions in the early 1900s. In its place the frontage of the school was extended to provide a school office and staff room on the first floor beneath which were cycle storage rooms and cloakrooms. Other extension work behind the building included the provision of a handicrafts and art room, classrooms and the creation of a preparatory school for boys between the ages of seven and ten. According to the book *The Story of a School* by the last headmaster, R.L. Chambers, a substantial amount of the money needed came from the sale of a colliery near Cannock.

A view towards the town centre looking up Lower High Street. On the left is the grammar school while on the right is the Scala Theatre, later to become known as the Savoy. With the demise of cinema in the face of TV competition, it closed and after a brief but unsuccessful spell as a supermarket it fell into disuse – and another of the street's many buildings began slowly to decay.

At the other end of the town, the Great Western Railway made its presence felt with road transport when it introduced bus services running to the Town and Junction stations and out as far as Hagley, Clent and Belbroughton. Here a double-decker bus leaves the town for Belbroughton. This picture was taken before the extension to St John's Road had been built. All the property on the left was demolished to make way for the ring road.

Looking up the High Street with the tram lines taking up much of the roadway, *c.* 1918. To the right and beyond some shops can be seen the frontage of the Talbot Hotel.

The Horse & Groom pub (above, right) is seen in about 1920, but was later demolished to make way for the extension of St John's Road from the edge of which the photograph below was taken. Several of the frontages were smartened up as Stourbridge became widely accepted throughout the Black Country and North Worcestershire as a slightly 'upmarket' town.

The distinctive façade of Mark & Moody Ltd's premises (above) brings back memories of a stationer's, bookseller's and printing business which had almost become a fixture and fitting of the High Street scene. Another equally well-known feature (below) was the huge display windows of J.H. Stringer Ltd, furnishers, based in the Commercial Buildings alongside which was built the Central (later the Odeon) Cinema.

Although some thirty years separate these two pictures, the then perceived stability of Stourbridge as a mid-to-upmarket shopping centre seemed indestructible. The corner of High Street and Foster Street (above) was dominated by the drapery and furnishing store of Joseph Jones (Eagle House) which extended over the equally well-known premises of Rutlands, wine merchants and shippers. Many families who owned or managed businesses in the town centre 'lived over the shop' (below). On the extreme right is the former Star Hotel, while further down is the sign of Mac Fisheries. 'Peplows Clock' remains a reminder of those days. Yet by the late 1980s the town centre's appeal had begun to fade; some say because of the competition from the Merry Hill Centre, others because of the civic pride lost when Stourbridge became part of the neighbouring Borough of Dudley.

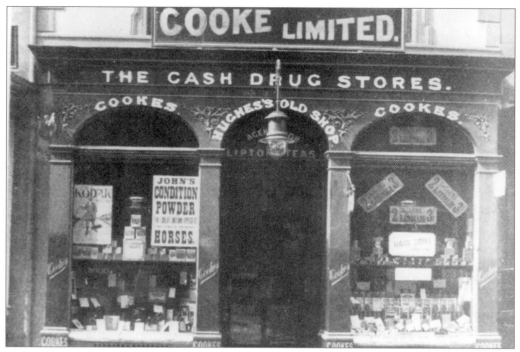

The exterior and interior of Cooke Ltd Cash Drug Stores (formerly Hughes's Old Shop). It retained its Victorian/Edwardian atmosphere, heralded by its distinctive frontage and confirmed inside by an array of bottles, jars, and products ranging from Lipton's tea to 'John's Condition Powder for Horses'.

Remember the phrase 'if you want to get ahead get a hat'? Dunham & Co. (above) of 121 High Street had one of the largest ranges of fashionable hats for men in North Worcestershire with an equally large array of men's shirts. Dowson's confectionery shop (below) was popular not only with patrons of the nearby Central (or Odeon) Cinema but was well known as a rather fashionable and civilized place to have morning coffee or afternoon tea.

North's butcher's shop, 63 High Street. Today this sight would send health inspectors into a frenzy! The North family were butchers in the town for over fifty years. To the left of the shop was the Coach & Horses which replaced a much earlier public house. The licensee was William Patch, described as 'a travelling showman'. He set up the Alhambra Theatre in Barlow's Yard which was at the rear of today's post office.

A.S. Price & Co. Ltd, dispensing chemists in the High Street, early 1950s. This firm owned a chain of drug stores throughout the Black Country and had their head office and warehouse at Corngreaves Road, Cradley Heath. The Fordson van and the Sunbeam Talbot car help to date this photograph.

Market Street also had a character all its own. These shops were demolished to make way for the Ryemarket shopping development. The well-known town photographer 'Hal' was also a retailer of perambulators and model aircraft – both from the shop next door to his studio. The *Express & Star* branch office later moved to Hagley Road, and then disappeared from the town altogether when it moved into the paper's regional office near Merry Hill.

Animals from Chipperfield's Circus (above and below). The circus was a regular visitor to the town and, if the weather was cold, water for the elephants was steam heated at Ashford's Dairy and taken to the animals by the circus fire engine.

Two town-centre based football teams. Above is the Stourbridge post office team of 1904/5 and, below, the Stourbridge Albion Football Club team based at the Duke William Hotel (Coventry Street), photographed shortly before a match against Cradley St Peter's in 1907.

Men from the local fire brigade, 1914. In 1879 Henry Turney decided to establish a volunteer fire brigade in the town and in 1880 a steam-powered fire pump was bought and housed in a fire station in Market Street; at one time the station's telephone number was Stourbridge 1. When the town hall was built a new fire station was also built at Smithfield, off Market Street and was opened by the Countess of Cambridge in 1926. In 1968 a new Worcestershire (now West Midlands) fire station was established at Parkfield Road. One of the biggest fires the old coal-fired steam pump fought was the blaze that gutted the central part of Enville Hall; the horse-drawn engine and its crew braved icy roads and a snow storm to get there. On the way the engine skidded into an icy ditch and the crew had to lever the engine back on to the road. Top: Joe Grant. Second row, left to right: Bert Nash, Bill Meredith, Joe Steele, George Banks, Bill Weaver and Driver George Whiteman. Front row: Tom Sidaway, Charlie Berry, -?-, Percy Harper, -?-, Capt. L. Walker, -?-, -?-, -?-, Bert Round.

Police Constable No. 3 Milner when he joined the Worcestershire Constabulary in 1904. In 1920 he was posted to Stourbridge from Himbleton, near Droitwich, where he had been the village bobby, and had served throughout the First World War. He had wanted to join the army but was ordered to remain in the police force. His early training as a mounted policeman stood him in good stead in Stourbridge when, on two occasions, he stopped horses that took fright and bolted down the High Street; on both occasions his chief constable presented him with a bravery award. He retired in 1928 and in that year his son Gerald started a greengrocery and general stores in the front room of the family home in Brook Street which he and his wife ran until they retired in 1991. During the Second World War Gerald Milner served with the 8th Army in North Africa and was with the 7th Armoured Division ('Desert Rats') during the decisive Battle of El Alamein.

Stourbridge town hall at the beginning of the twentieth century. This replaced the original town hall (or market house) which was demolished in 1773 to widen the road in the town centre. The new town hall was built on the site of a former corn exchange to celebrate Queen Victoria's Jubilee and was opened in 1887 by Lord Beauchamp (Lord Lieutenant of Worcestershire). While construction was in progress the town commissioners decided to add a new corn exchange, council chamber, offices and a fire station, which were all opened in 1888. The canopy over the Market Street entrance was removed some time earlier this century. The old Institute Building (left) presented a more austere frontage.

One of the earliest known photographs of Market Street (above), believed to have been taken in the late nineteenth century. Market Street was originally known as Ryemarket. The front of the town hall can be seen on the extreme left, while the property on the right was later demolished and the road widened with new retail premises being built. At the end of Market Street the outline of the Old Bank can just be made out. The wider Market Street and a variety of shops (below) soon became a quality shopping area equal to that of the High Street. To the left is the 'new' Stourbridge Institute building which was opened in 1937.

Ashford's started with a milk float on 1 May 1922 and grew to become one of the largest independent and family owned companies, dominating Stourbridge's commercial life for sixty-three years. The founder, Ronald Ashford, began with a horse and milk float and used to collect his milk from a farm at Bell End, near Bromsgrove. Twelve months later he was joined by his brother Edward who had previously run a cycle shop. In 1927 the third brother, Bernard (a Cook's travel agent), joined them. The shop seen here traded under the name of Ashford Bros in High Street, Stourbridge for many years. Buying ice-cream manufacturing equipment in a bankruptcy sale, the Ashford brothers broke fresh ground for they were possibly the first company to cash in by having ice-cream sales outlets at many cinemas. Such was the success of this venture – as 'Blue Boy Ice Cream' – that the 'big boys' such as Walls and Lyons muscled in and gained control of ice-cream sales in most of the major cinema chains of the 1930s. In the 1930s the company changed its name to Ashford Dairies and, after the Second World War, to Ashford Creameries. In the 1960s the company also founded Fiesta Foods and continued to flourish until eventually being taken over by a national group in 1985, when the family link ended.

This enormous tricycle (above), without gears!, was used to deliver dairy products around the area; those employees who used it were said to have the strongest legs in the locality. Before the widespread use of motor transport for local deliveries, this horse and milk float (below) was a regular sight in Stourbridge and district.

The first suggestion for public baths in Stourbridge was made in 1886 but it was not until 1900 that plans were drawn up by Frederick Woodward, with the new baths being opened in May 1901. Within a month the Stourbridge Swimming Club was founded and a month later a ladies' swimming club came into existence. In 1923 an open-air pool was opened with the indoor baths being modernized in 1939. Swimming was regarded as a summer sport in those days, and during the winter months the indoor pool area was covered and the hall used for meetings, dances and an indoor cricket school. The whole complex was demolished, together with the nearby Territorial Army headquarters in Bell Street, to make way for the Crystal Leisure Centre.

A postcard view of the public library at the junction of Church Street and Hagley Road. The library was opened in 1905 thanks in no small measure to a £3,000 grant from the American philanthropist, Andrew Carnegie. It occupied the ground floor with the art and technical school occupying the first floor. The top floor was used as a girls' secondary school which, in 1928, became the new County High School for Girls at Junction Road. This picture was taken before St John's Road had been extended beyond Foster Street to join the High Street by Weaver's Garage, to the left. At the outbreak of the Second World War the garage was converted to a British restaurant and, after closing in 1949, became a fruit, vegetable and fish market known locally as 'Housewives Corner'. This, together with the distinctive buildings on the right, was pulled down to make way for the ring road.

Stourbridge war memorial was erected in 1923 to honour those who gave their lives in the First World War. It cost £3,000 and was unveiled by the Earl of Coventry (Lord Lieutenant of Worcestershire). The memorial was later moved to Mary Stevens Park where a rededication ceremony was held.

The High Street, early 1900s. The Talbot Hotel (right) was the major venue for events on the town's social calendar. Formerly the home of the Foley family, the building dates back to the seventeenth century. It was also the principal hotel in the area catering for visiting businessmen and has always been the meeting place of the town's Rotary Club, which was founded in 1922, as well as a number of other professional bodies.

The thriving livestock market, Parkfield Road, *c.* 1910. Despite its proximity to the Black Country, Stourbridge retained more than a slight air of a country market town. The site is now occupied by the fire station. In the background can be seen St John's Church, built in 1860 at a cost of £4,000.

Infantrymen, led by the band of the Worcestershire Regiment, march up the High Street towards the station en route to the trenches of France, 1914. For many it was farewell for ever to Stourbridge.

This tank, a veteran of the French battlefields, was placed in a special enclosure at the junction of Greenfield Avenue and Heath Street as a reminder of the First World War. Ironically it was removed, broken up and melted down in the call for scrap metal as the Second World War loomed.

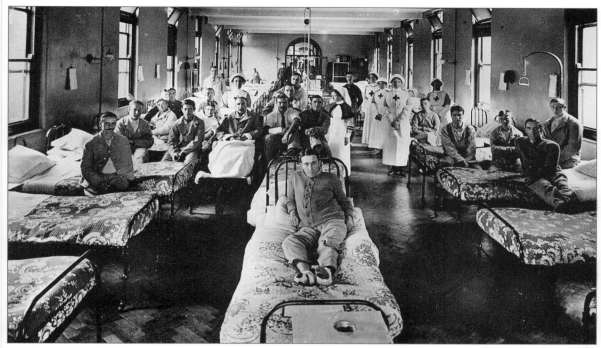

It was not long before the horrors of the trenches came to Stourbridge and district. Scores of injured soldiers regularly arrived in Stourbridge by ambulance train to be taken to local hospitals for treatment.

The former Sandfield workhouse, later used as a hospital. So many wounded soldiers were being brought back from France that throughout England existing hospitals could not cope and other buildings were requisitioned and turned either into hospitals or recovery units.

Wounded soldiers and the nursing staff in the grounds of Studley Court during a summer's afternoon, 1916. This was another house used as a hospital; it later became the Stourbridge Borough Council offices in Mary Stevens Park.

The advent of the Second World War resulted in a recruiting drive for special constables. There was no shortage of men above military age who volunteered to serve and this photograph, taken in 1944, was of many of those 'specials' who served alongside the Worcestershire Constabulary in Stourbridge and Halesowen. There are nearly 100 'specials' of all ranks seen here, among whom have been identified Albert Pimlott, Alex Shear (front row, sixth and seventh from left) and Wilfred Hill (fourth row, twelfth from left).

The magnificent assembly hall of King Edward VI School, Stourbridge with seating for over 600 pupils. It was opened in 1931 and during construction work it was reported that what was believed to have been the remains of the old chantry dating back to 1430, which also formed the original school, had been uncovered. In the assembly hall one wall carried honours boards listing the academic successes of its pupils at the nation's leading universities. In 1948 an organ was installed and tablets were mounted on the front of the balcony (left) to form the school's memorial to those old boys killed in the Second World War.

Stourbridge County High School for Girls began life as a secondary school for girls in 1905, although in 1871 there had been a proposal to found a girls' grammar school in the town. The school was opened in 1929 by the Duchess of Atholl (as minister for education) and was administered by governors representing Worcestershire and Staffordshire County Councils, Stourbridge Borough Council and Birmingham University as well as co-opted members. With the demise of grammar schools locally, it became Red Hill School taking pupils from the ages of eleven to sixteen. A previous independent school of the same name had closed down several years before.

Close to the town centre was another private school, Alexandra House School for Girls (above and below). Although it closed many years ago and was later converted into flats, its distinctive design dominates the junction of Enville Street and the ring road.

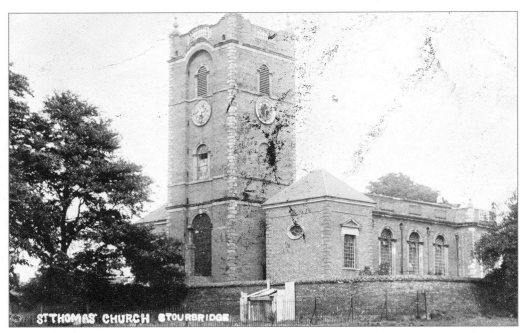

The parish church encompassing Stourbridge town is St Thomas's in Market Street (above). Strangely the bell tower is at the far end of the church from Market Street. Building work began in 1728 and was completed in 1736, its interior being noted for its fine Georgian decoration and design. For a time during the eighteenth century various vicars also combined the duties of headmaster of King Edward's School – an arrangement which seemed to cause some friction according to Mr Chambers's book on the school's history. St Thomas's Scout Group (below) was one of the largest and most successful in the area and is seen here (date unknown) with the Gamage Challenge Shield; exactly what the shield was awarded for is unknown.

The interior (above) of Stourbridge Roman Catholic Church, New Road. The church was built in 1865 and a 130 ft spire added in 1889. However, the church was not consecrated until 9 July 1891. Greenfield Avenue (below) was, towards the end of the nineteenth century, the favourite place for the town's professional people to own houses. Despite being an access and exit route for the ring road, it still retains much of the charm of a bygone era. The Catholic church spire can be seen in the background.

Greenfield Gardens at the junction of Heath Street and Greenfield Avenue were bought for the town and opened as pleasure gardens in 1903 with the bandstand being given by Walter Jones, a former chairman of Stourbridge Urban District Council and proprietor of Jones & Attwood, Engineers of Amblecote. The site of the gardens now is merely a grassed area and a few trees – a sorry sight when compared with these pictures taken earlier in the twentieth century.

Although originally in Amblecote – the smallest urban district council in the UK until it was split up and divided between Stourbridge Borough and Dudley County Borough – Corbett Hospital began life as a private Georgian house, The Hill, within a 30-acre estate. It was originally owned by Brierley Hill-born John Corbett, who became a millionaire with his 'rediscovery' of the salt deposits of Droitwich where he soon became known as 'The Salt King'. He built a house in Droitwich, Château Impney, of classical French château design, for his French-born bride. But legend has it that she so disliked the place that she never lived there. He presented his Amblecote house to the trustees in 1893 (together with a £20,000 endowment) for use as an eighteen-bed hospital. It was opened as such in 1893 by Viscountess Cobham and over the ensuing years expanded to include more wards, an outpatients' department, nurses' home and nurses' training school. Currently there is a campaign to reinstate its accident and emergency unit on the grounds that the nearest such unit is several miles away at Dudley.

Before the creation of a National Health Service, Corbett Hospital, like all hospitals, raised much of its finance through public efforts and donations. Therefore, the hospital's annual fêtes became major events in the district. These two pictures are of two 'floats' arriving back in the hospital grounds after having paraded through Stourbridge and Amblecote accompanied by supporters armed with collecting boxes.

For many years Mary Stevens Park was the jewel in the crown of many public open spaces and gardens presented to Stourbridge by wealthy industrialists and landowners. But, as Studley Court, it very nearly became a housing development area. In 1927 the Cradley Heath industrialist, Ernest Stevens, bought the house and land and, on 20 December 1929, he presented it to the Borough of Stourbridge in memory of his wife, Mary. This picture was taken at the presentation by Mr Stevens to the Mayor of Stourbridge, Alderman H.E. Palfrey. Eventually the house became the borough council offices and a council chamber was built alongside with the gardens, lake, bowling greens and tennis courts always kept in pristine condition. As a result of local government reorganization Stourbridge became part of the Dudley Metropolitan Borough and over the years the park has lost much of its former splendour.

Mary Stevens Park gates (above) are styled on those of Buckingham Palace and are now protected by a Grade II listing. The gardens nearest the gates remain popular with newly weds for wedding photographs. Pictured below, shortly after the park was opened to the public, the neat avenue of trees and well-tended flower beds give a flavour of the park's former glories.

Two more views of Mary Stevens Park in its heyday. The bandstand (above) was host to some of the best in music from local town bands and orchestras as well as military bands and a few concerts are still held there during summer months. The superb bowling greens (below) were surrounded by well-tended flower beds beyond which were large expanses of grassed areas.

Even the youngsters were well catered for in Mary Stevens Park; apart from swings, slides and roundabouts there was also a large paddling pool and other play areas.

Overlooking the park is the former Studley Court, pictured after the parkland had been given to Stourbridge. Previously it had been owned by a number of prominent local industrialists and business families among them being Rufford, Cochrane, Turney and Webb. Today the building houses part of the engineering and highways department of Dudley Metropolitan Borough Council.

Mary Stevens Park was also a popular venue for picnic parties hosted by local organizations. A group of members from the Stourbridge Liberal Unionist Association (above) shortly after the park's opening. It was also the natural place for Stourbridge town's carnival processions to end their tour of the district (below).

It is hard to equate this scene (above) of the junction of New Road and Worcester Street with today's mayhem of traffic on the ring road. This postcard scene is thought to date from about 1920 and was taken from the mouth of Market Street with children able to gather round the lamppost in the centre of the crossroads without a vehicle in sight! Equally deserted is the junction of Worcester Street and Heath Lane (below) near the entrance to Mary Stevens Park. It is equally hard to visualize that there was once a glass works to the right of this photograph.

Cranage's delivery cart (above) thought to be in Love Lane, *c.* 1900. Cranage's bakery in Stourbridge used to deliver to a wide area of Stourbridge, particularly in the Norton and Pedmore areas. Of a more powerful nature was the traction engine (below) belonging to Simeon Bateman's timber yard in Union Street, Stourbridge; the machine was a regular sight around Stourbridge as it hauled tree trunks and loads of sawn timber to and from the sawmills.

One of the earliest 'taxi' services in Stourbridge was operated by Mr Len Bingham, seen here with his wife standing in front of one of his horse-drawn cabs. He was also a parcel carrier and was a well-known visitor as far afield as Hagley, Clent and Kinver.

A well-known industrial firm in Stourbridge was that of B. Fiddian & Son Ltd, spade, shovel, fork and agricultural implement manufacturers of Albion Works, Brook Street, Stourbridge. The founder of the company was well known in various professional bodies in the locality and the firm's 'Celebrated Albion Brand' products were sold nationwide as well as exported. Among those seen here are Reg Timmins, George Smith, May Beasley, Jack Willetts, George Timmins, Lily Yates and Mr Evans (foreman).

On the outskirts of all towns corner shops abounded and were an important part of domestic life. Two such shops are seen here. Above is the Dawes's family shop, 1 Clifton Street, confectioners and general stores; the person standing in the doorway is thought to be Mrs May Dawes with her children Ralph (six) and Eric (nine). Below is Haynes stores of Western Road in 1930 with Mr Vic Haynes and his son Roger in the doorway. The two houses next door were later used as furniture showrooms.

Many of the roads leading out from Stourbridge towards Hagley, Kidderminster and Bridgnorth were tree lined, particularly in the Norton area. Above is a postcard (early 1900s) of South Avenue while, below, the well-tended trees bordering South Road at about the same time provide a tranquil setting – a marked contrast with today!

Examples of the labyrinth of side streets in the older part of Norton are seen here with Heath Street (above) and Clifton Street (below). The latter street had its own sub-post office which shared the same premises with a butcher's. Today both streets are packed with parked cars as few of the houses have off-road parking.

Yet another example of the rural aspect of Stourbridge's fringes is evident from this postcard looking up Norton Road at the turn of the twentieth century. The large houses on the left were usually hidden from public view by trees and shrubs, while on the right there was open farmland. Today Norton Road is completely built up with a range of properties, some over 100 years old.

The Mere Cottage Homes (now demolished) at Norton were established to provide security for older local children who had been deprived for various reasons of a normal home life. The homes were built in 1904.

A building which has survived three changes of use, considerable internal structural change and one fire is the former Star & Garter public house at the junction of Heath Lane and Norton Road. The pub's former livery stable can be seen here, to the left. After it closed as a public house it was converted into a wine bar and disco much to the annoyance of local people. But after a somewhat chequered though short-lived period it was badly damaged by fire. It is now part of a national newsagents and minimarket chain.

An artist's drawing of Norton Mission Church at about the time it was opened. Although details of the building are sparse, it is thought to have been the predecessor of St Michael's and All Angels Church which was opened in 1929.

This early picture of Stanley Road, which runs alongside Mary Stevens Park, shows only one house with two houses on the skyline in Love Lane.

Shortly before leaving Stourbridge (and what was Worcestershire) to enter Staffordshire (albeit for only about a mile) is the Greyhound Inn at the junction of Greyhound Lane, seen here at the turn of the twentieth century. The pub and the adjoining cottages were demolished several years ago and a new public house with the same name (but, say the locals, not the same atmosphere) was built.

Right on the border with Staffordshire – which is marked by a bridleway – lies Norton Covert. A former sandpit, the Covert is now heavily wooded and has been an ideal and safe playground for generations of local children and a pleasant area for an afternoon or summer's evening stroll. Today several of its paths have been taken over (illegally) by mountain bikers who have erected various obstacles to test their skills. It was acquired by Stourbridge Borough Council and is now controlled by Dudley Metropolitan Borough Council.

Of all roads leading into Stourbridge the most impressive and pleasing to the eye is Hagley Road, seen here in the 1920s. The large bay windows of the building on the left were garage showrooms of what became Apex Motors (Ford dealers) then Jessups and later Bristol Street. Next door the protruding building and other property belonged to the Austin dealership of Stour Valley Motor Company (now part of the Lex Group). In both cases the original buildings have been demolished to make way for modern showrooms and forecourt sales areas. However, most of the property beyond has remained largely unaltered.

Looking away from town along the Hagley Road the street scene has changed little (except for traffic!). To the left the Swan Hotel and, next door, the imposing frontage of the county court and the properties beyond have altered very little. To the extreme right can be seen what was Green's grocery store, famed for its home-roasted coffee beans. Close by was Kemps, a small confectionery shop and café.

In Hagley Road stands Stourbridge's second oldest school, Oldswinford Hospital, formerly known as the Bluecoats (above). Now an independent school, it was founded in 1667 by the local ironmaster, Thomas Foley. With the demise of King Edward VI School as a grammar school, Oldswinford Hospital School underwent a rapid expansion in facilities and pupil numbers. It now maintains one of the highest scholastic achievement records of any school in the country. Pictured below, in the early 1900s, is this parade of the boys in their distinctively styled blue uniforms which gave them the name of 'Bluecoats'.

For centuries St Mary's Church was the parish church of Stourbridge and there has been a church at Oldswinford since 1285. Although the tower is late fourteenth century, the nave of St Mary's was rebuilt in 1842 and a new chancel was built in 1898. For many years the annual Charter Day service of King Edward VI School was held there with the pupils marching through the town to Oldswinford. It had many notable rectors one of whom, according to a borough council guide book, 'was C.H. Craufurd who achieved notoriety by marrying his cook and then preached about it'. The church was restored in 1938 by Sir Charles Scott RA, who also designed the gateway and churchyard walls. The spire, erected in 1809/10, was eventually deemed unsafe and was dismantled in 1985. Mr Fred Hayward, who drove Stourbridge Council's last horse-drawn cart and then, prior to retirement, took responsibility for keeping the main streets of Oldswinford and Pedmore tidy, is seen here.

St Mary's Parish Church choir members and church officials pictured outside the rectory, 1906. The rectory (below), an elegant Georgian building, was built in the eighteenth century and replaced a much older building. During the Second World War it was used by troops and in 1947 the new rector, the Canon A.V. Hurley, had substantial repairs carried out – and, at the same time, had several 'add-on' buildings demolished.

Oldswinford parish church, being the original parish church of Stourbridge, has always featured in civic and other important events in Stourbridge and was frequently the venue for the borough's annual civic service. This photograph is of the civic procession during the mayoralty of Alderman H.E. Palfrey. Others in the picture include the Mace Bearer and Mayor's Attendant, Sgt Major Goodyear, Alderman Frank Leeson and the Stourbridge MP, Mr R.H. Morgan (Conservative).

St Mary's Church fête was one of the major events in the Oldswinford social calendar as this picture (above) shows, *c.* 1912. Oldswinford Castle (below), now a block of flats one floor of which has been built into the roof, is one of the oldest buildings in the area. Originally a Tudor-style, half-timbered building (it was never a 'true' castle), its origins are thought to date back to the fifteenth century. Numerous rebuilds and renovations now hide its true antiquity. It was once owned by the Hickman family who were closely connected with the cloth trade of Stourbridge.

Most of the side roads around the original centre of Oldswinford were tree lined but many of those avenues of trees were removed as roads were widened and housing development spread outwards. One road which has retained its appearance of 100 years ago or more is Church Road (above) viewed from the church. The Georgian building on the left, Swinford Old Hall, later known as The Laurels, became a home for the elderly in 1951. Closed in recent years, there are plans to convert it into apartments. At the other end of Church Road (below), the buildings to the right complete with their lancet-style windows still survive, while behind the trees on the left lay Oldswinford Castle, the extensive gardens of which became a small housing development.

Houses (above) near Oldswinford crossroads, 1911. This block of houses remains much the same today, as does Glasshouse Hill (below). The Labour In Vain public house can be seen at the junction with Red Hill. In the distance can be seen the locomotive water tower at the Junction station.

Oldswinford School (above) was opened in the 1850s and, apart from much of the main building being constructed in Staffordshire blue brick, the school's external appearance was unusual in that it had a distinctive bell tower and coloured tiles forming a patterned roof. The school was demolished to make way for housing. A group of pupils (below) with their teacher in about 1910. Note the slate which recalls the days when the area was called 'Old Swinford'.

Another example of Oldswinford's retention of many of its older buildings. Oakley's was a combined confectioners, bakery and grocery store and was probably the biggest store outside Stourbridge town in what was essentially a village when this photograph was taken. It had horse-drawn delivery vans and a state-of-the-art motor van. Today the buildings are occupied by Asian fast-food premises, an off-licence and a video-film hire library. The shopping area on the other side of the crossroads (below) is still relatively unchanged from this picture of 1920.

For some years Oldswinford also had a steam laundry (above), although no records seem to exist providing details of the firm's history. A winter's scene (below) with cows being herded from Love Lane into what is now Swinford Road. The lane ahead led to a public footpath across farmland which is now occupied by housing.

Mary Stevens Maternity Home, Hagley Road, Oldswinford after building work was completed in 1932. It was yet another gift from Ernest Stevens and was built on the site of an older building which Mr Stevens had intended to convert into a maternity home in memory of his wife. But when he was told the building was unsuitable for conversion he gave orders for it to be demolished and had a purpose-built home erected on the site. The twenty-four-bed home was opened in September 1932 by the Minister of Health, Sir E. Hilton Young (later Baron Kennet of Dene). Today its grounds are used in part by the Mary Stevens Hospice, while the former maternity home is used by a number of voluntary bodies, not all of which are based within the former Borough of Stourbridge.

Beyond Oldswinford lies Pedmore, once a small community clustered round an ancient church, St Peter's. The old church was taken down and a new one built in about 1869. Remains of the original church – notably the arch of the south door – date from the twelfth century. Below is a view of the altar, choir stalls and pulpit from about 1920.

Pedmore Parish Hall (above) was erected in memory of a former rector (the Revd J.H. Whiteley) by his widow on land in the centre of the old village. The hall, known as the parish rooms, was designed by Mr T. Grazebrook and built on land donated by Mr J.B. Cochrane. It was opened on 16 December 1902. Before the expansion of housing, this scene (below) was typical of the countryside around Pedmore and Wollescote.

# WOLLASTON

*Despite being barely a mile from Stourbridge town centre and with no clear boundary line between the two, Wollaston has always retained its separate identity. Even today the centre of Wollaston is commonly referred to as 'The Village'. It was also an important junction of two tramway routes: one from Stourbridge and the other, the Kinver Light Railway, from the Fish Inn, Amblecote, going forward to Stourton and the terminus in Mill Lane, Kinver. This picture was taken in 1909, where the actual junction is now covered by the traffic island.*

A funeral cortège of trams (above) stops the traffic in Wollaston, 22 January 1915. The funeral was that of the Revd E.G. Hexall, who had founded 'Bethany' at The Hyde, Kinver, a home for crippled children who had been abandoned by their parents. After a service at the Providence Chapel, Oldbury, interment followed at Spon Lane Cemetery. The cortège (below) was formed by two tram cars and a wagon which had been converted into a bier and is pictured here on a 'passing loop' at Darby's Farm, Stourton while it waited for a Kinver-bound tram to pass.

High Park Avenue, Wollaston

Even today, High Park Avenue is a pleasant tree-lined road. This picture (above) from the early 1920s features the Gate Hangs Well public house with an ornate lamp over its doorway. Below is a photograph of the pub's bowling club members; the green is now occupied by the pub's car park.

A well-known Wollaston business at the turn of the century was that of Langstone's of 55 High Street. This general business was owned by Francis and Harriet Langstone; the delivery cart (above) was pulled by their horse 'Old Will'. Langstone's also appeared to be involved in the haulage business with 'Old Will' about to leave the shop's rear yard (below).

James Pearsall's bakery and shop in Mamble Road, lying on the border of Wollaston and Stourbridge, *c.* 1905. An intriguing sign in the window reads 'Bermaline Bread, Montgomerie's Patent' (whatever that was!). The lady in the doorway is believed to be Mrs Pearsall.

Built in 1860, Wollaston parish church is a handsome structure of blue brick with stone dressing and in the Early English style. The church, school and the master's house were the gift of Stourbridge ironmaster, William Orme Foster, who 'liberally endowed the church'. Mr Foster also paid for the building of the vicarage. The school buildings have now been demolished and the land used for housing.

The main shopping area of Wollaston is in Bridgnorth Road and most of the buildings have changed little since this picture (above) was taken in the 1920s. A small island (left) had a signpost, while to the right an open area of land is now a car park. The newsagent's shop was owned by Charles Smalley. In the 1950s it was owned by a Mr Cooper who was followed into the business by his son. Further along the row was Mr Hawkeswood's chemist's shop. Below, a picture of roughly the same period shows the view up Bridgnorth Road and part of the tramway junction.

An interesting picture of three buses in Wollaston village centre (possibly taken in Meriden Avenue), *c.* 1918. Regular bus services began in the Stourbridge area in April 1914 but even so it was not until 1930 that the tram services ended. The Birmingham & Midland Motor Omnibus Co. (more popularly known as the Midland Red) soon became involved in a fierce battle with Samuel Johnson's 'Supreme' buses for passengers and resorted to running one bus in front and another behind the Johnson bus in order to corner the passenger market. The Midland Red was also involved in competition with a Wollaston-based firm, believed to be called 'Grey Coaches' and it is said one of the Wollaston drivers became so incensed that he pulled a Midland Red driver from his cab and hit him! Needless to say Midland Red won the day and soon had a complete monopoly of services.

The Albion Inn, Withy Bank, at the turn of the twentieth century. It had an interesting history in that it featured, in company with several other public houses, in a legal battle between two breweries. In the centre is the licensee, Mary Kendrick and presumably the girl by her side was her daughter. The story is that the Swan Brewery of Quarry Bank (founded in 1857) was registered as Home Brewery (Quarry Bank) Ltd in 1903 to acquire twenty-three pubs owned by J.P. Simpkiss. A subsequent lawsuit in 1916 resulted in Simpkiss losing control – a puzzling situation in that Simpkiss's had been the company taken over. The Albion Inn closed in 1921 and the property was demolished in 1959.

In the early years of the twentieth century, the Goodhead family owned this typical villa house turned general stores in Enville Street and close to Mamble Road. Mrs Goodhead is the lady with the white apron with, it is thought, Mr Goodhead in the doorway.

Formerly known as The Crescent, this lawned area with gardens is now the car park at the junction of Meriden Avenue and Bridgnorth Road, Wollaston. Note the horse water trough presented by the RSPCA.

Still standing and not having changed very much in appearance over the past seventy-five years is the former corn mill which is at the junction of Vicarage Road and High Street, Wollaston. Today it is an antiques centre.

Edkins Depositories, *c.* 1912. The man driving the two-handed cart was Mr G.H. Richards and the piebald mare was 'Maggie'. In 1924 the property changed hands and became Wollaston Garages.

Wollaston Garage when it was a Morris and (according to the sign) Wolseley commercial dealership, 1945. The lorry belonged to Bill Potter, a coal merchant of Lower High Street, Stourbridge.

Two years after opening (1924) the Wollaston Garage premises were gutted by fire with only the house remaining intact. According to contemporary press reports, it was the biggest fire ever seen in Wollaston.

The burnt-out remains in the workshop were of a six-cylinder Essex car (made in America). When modernization work took place an old inspection pit was uncovered and in it was found one of the wheels of this old car. The house, which survived the blaze and now forms the offices of Wollaston Garages, was the home of the Haynes family who still own the garage. It is thought the business must be one of the oldest in England to still be owned and operated by the family who founded it over seventy years ago.

A Reed Tooby employee departs by motorcycle combination with a delivery of material for a contract, *c. 1922*. For many years this firm was well known in the Wollaston and Stourbridge areas. Founded in the late nineteenth century in Enville Street, the Tooby family were closely involved with the borough's development with Capt E.R.R. Tooby becoming Mayor in 1951–2.

In the 1930s West Street Methodist School hall was the venue for the popular Mothers and Babies Club, its members coming from Wollaston and Stourbridge.

One of the most imposing houses in the area was Wollaston Hall. A fine half-timbered building which had undergone a number of structural alterations and extensions in its lifetime, its precise age was unknown. However, the date 1617 was found carved in one of its oak beams. It was damaged by fire and the remainder of the building was dismantled and shipped to America in the mid-1920s.

Two of Wollaston Hall's staff pictured by what appears to be a lodge house belonging to the hall. The hall was occupied by many prominent families among them being the Addenbrookes, one of whose number, John, founded the famous hospital at Cambridge that bears his family name. Below is a view along the tree-lined avenue leading to the hall. The access to the hall was off High Street, Wollaston, roughly where Apley Road is now constructed.

Scouts, believed to have been from Wollaston, in camp. The location of the camp is unknown, but a popular area for Scout activity in the area was on farmland where Eggington Road now stands and this picture may have been taken there. The Scoutmaster is believed to be a member of the Tooby family.

Eighty years ago at a time of little if any transport fumes it was not unusual to see sides of meat hung up outside butchers' premises, as seen here in Enville Street. The location is thought to be in the vicinity of today's Army & Navy Stores.

The Dulson family's butcher's shop in High Street, Wollaston, *c.* 1930. It was also a wet fish shop and later became a ladies' hairdressing salon.

The Plough public house in Bridgnorth Road, Wollaston. This building remains one of the most popular in the village and has changed little from when it was first built; for many years the licence remained with the same family.

Away from their classrooms, pupils of Wollaston's St James's School celebrate the coronation of King George V with a party on the school's lawn.

Wollaston Infants School pupils celebrated the coronation by entering this float and joining in the street procession around Wollaston. It would appear from the picture that the starting point of the procession was High Park Road.

At the turn of the twentieth century Wollaston had a close affinity with the farming community for, apart from Enville Street, High Street and part of Bridgnorth Road, the rest of the land was almost all agricultural. These two scenes were typical of the haymaking season when everyone, including mothers and children, went into the fields to help with the harvesting. Note the horse driver who, despite the summer's day, was wearing a waistcoat, a starched collar and a tie.

High Park Farm, Wollaston, at the turn of the twentieth century. One of the largest farms in the district, it stood part way along on the right of what is now High Park Road. The whole of the farm's land now forms a vast area of housing and Ridgewood School grounds.

This picture (above) is captioned merely as 'Cross Roads', but it has been suggested that it is in fact an unmade track which is now High Park Avenue looking towards Wollaston with High Park Farm buildings on the left and houses in Wollaston on the horizon (right). The cross roads referred to may have been the junction of Dunsley Road, Sandy Lane (Roman Road) and South Road. The authors would be grateful for any information which could precisely identify this view. The milk float (below) belonged to John Darby of High Park Farm who operated a substantial milk delivery service in the district.

This splendid photograph is said to be of a Mr Weaver who was a chauffeur. But to whom? The location is also debatable but is probably outside a house in Wood Street, Wollaston, which was thought to have been a small dairy. There was a Mr Weaver who was also chauffeur at Enville Hall, near Kinver.

An organized outing for regular customers from the Unicorn Inn, early 1900s. One cannot help but feel sorry for the horse on the left who had to pull a carriage on which there were at least ten passengers, whereas the other carriage had two horses. The Unicorn's licence remained in the same family (the Billinghams) for a period of eighty years. This pub began its life in the mid-1850s when a Wordsley foundry mould-maker named Joseph Lakin, also a noted bare-fist boxer (a pugilist), decided to augment his income by becoming an inn keeper – thanks to 'King Billy's Beerhouse Bill'. Apparently, King William IV, aided by the Duke of Wellington, felt that ex-pugilists and soldiers would make ideal licensees once their previous active lifestyle had ended. But because very few had ever made enough money to buy an established licence they had been reduced to begging or theft to survive. King William's act enabled such people to brew their own beer for a nominal licence and turn their own homes into beer houses.

# AMBLECOTE

*Amblecote has made its history in several ways. It was mentioned, albeit briefly, in the Domesday Book when, in 1086, it had a population of seven. As its name suggests it possibly goes back to Saxon times. In more recent times it became famed as the nation's centre of glassmaking. In addition its history of ironworking and coal mining was aided by the arrival of the Stourbridge Canal in 1779, which meant its products could be carried cheaply and reliably throughout England and, via such waterways as the River Severn, to the ports. In 1894 it elected a parish council of eleven members and later became an urban district council which, covering a mere 665 acres – not much more than a large farm – gained fame as the smallest urban district council in England. In 1966, a reorganization of local government divided it between Brierley Hill Urban District Council and Stourbridge Borough Council. Eventually, both Brierley Hill and Stourbridge were amalgamated with Dudley to form Dudley Metropolitan Borough Council.*
*For many years the Hewitt family were well-known garage proprietors in Amblecote. Their new garage (seen here) was opened in the High Street (roughly where a joinery store now stands) and its striking art deco frontage and plate-glass window patterns attracted widespread attention.*

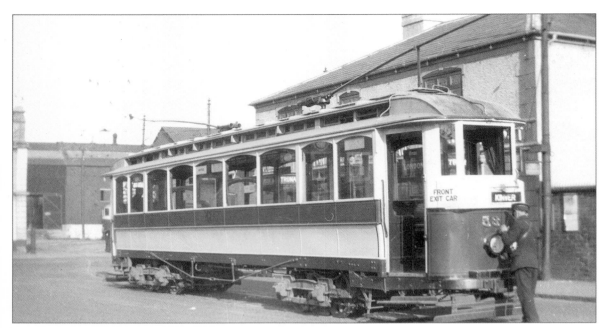

The traditional centre of Amblecote was the Fish crossroads named after the pub (now an oriental food restaurant) that stood at the junction of Stourbridge Road and the Wollaston Road. It was also known to tens of thousands of day trippers as where the Kinver Light Railway (a tramway) began its journey to Kinver. In the early 1900s, 30,000 people used the Kinver trams at Amblecote one Whitsuntide bank holiday weekend with trams running every seven minutes to bring the trippers back from Kinver. Car no. 53 (above) is being prepared for a trip to Kinver. In the company's depot yard (below) is a semi-open car built at Tividale in 1916. The depot was on the opposite side of Stourbridge Road to the Fish Inn.

There were many public houses at the Amblecote crossroads. On the opposite side of the Stourbridge Road to the Fish Inn was the Glassmaker's Arms, while on the other side of the Wollaston Road stood the Little Pig. Although the former has been demolished and replaced by a statue commemorating the area's glassmaking heritage, the Little Pig still survives. It replaced an old pub of the same name, the new one being built in 1930 by T. W. Edwards & Sons (Audnam) Ltd. It was during demolition of the old pub that a box was found containing a large collection of glass photographic negatives which are now in the custody of the Edwards family. The licensee at the time of rebuilding was Mr W.M. Hawkins.

Foundrymen and 'lads' from the Stewkins, Audnam, foundry of Henry Robinson's in the mid-1930s. The firm's main products were cast-iron gutters and pipe work.

Even in the 1920s motorcycles were not the sole domain of men. Pictured astride a motorcycle combination is Mrs Evelyn Lowe with her sister-in-law Barbara in the sidecar holding baby 'Mags'.

Men in the machine shop at the works of Isaac Nash & Sons Ltd, a firm of general ironworkers and agricultural implement manufacturers. They also had a second works at Belbroughton. Identified in the picture is Reginald Hill (third from left) and James Hill, possibly the foreman (second from the right).

This scene is described as Lower Brettel Lane on this early postcard. Note the tram from Dudley which had an open-top deck and which had apparently come to a standstill for the benefit of the photographer.

Possibly the ultimate in property-owning 'one-upmanship'. This photograph was in the form of a postcard probably commissioned by the new owner to tell his/her friends of the family's new address!

The Stourbridge Canal provided a welcome boost to the growing industry of Amblecote, Wordsley and district. The Amblecote works of E.J. & J. Pearson Ltd, firebrick manufacturers, made considerable use of the waterway to ship their products to many parts of England, including London, the East Midlands, Yorkshire and the North West. Their wharves were invariably filled with narrow boats being loaded with up to 30 tons of bricks and other products.

With the competition of rail and then road transport the canals fell into disrepair and some became derelict. However, in the 1960s they were 'rediscovered' by a new kind of boat – the holiday cruiser – and here is one such boat descending the sixteen locks at Wordsley. In the background the only surviving glassworks' cone is seen beyond Dadford's Shed, a former transhipment warehouse and now a flourishing boat-building and repair yard. The whole of the lock flight has been turned into a conservation area.

Looking up Brettell Lane towards Brierley Hill (above) with the only traffic being a tramcar and a horse and cart, *c.* 1915. Much of the property on the left was demolished in later years. However, the picture below, taken, judging from the alignment of road kerbstones, from roughly the same spot some twenty years later on, shows that many of the properties had extended outwards as shop fronts. Several of the shopkeepers are standing outside their premises for the benefit of the photographer. One of the traders was (centre) the local barber, Mr Hazeldine. On the extreme left can be seen part of Moody's butcher's shop.

Wordsley canal junction was not merely busy with working boats heading to and from the River Severn at Stourport but at weekends it was a favourite weekend venue for steamer trips either up to Stourbridge or down to Stourton Locks and Kinver. Both the Stourbridge Navigation Company houses seen here have long since been demolished. Beyond the bridge (above) can be seen the first of the sixteen locks which lift the canal up through Wordsley.

Master craftsman Henry Lown (right) working on the refurbishment of a glass kiln, *c.* 1930. Mr Lown died in 1941 aged seventy-eight. The identity of his assistants is not known.

Stuart's glass cone is seen in the centre, while to the left is the Whitehouse cone and a third unidentified cone beyond, 1920s. Glasswork cones were once a feature of the Amblecote and Wordsley skyline. To the left of the picture the roadside railings still exist and immediately beyond them there was a road (now known as Junction Road) leading to some factories.

A network of scaffolding surrounds the Whitehouse glass house during maintenance work. This cone was dismantled in 1938.

Stourbridge Cricket Club was founded in the 1868 and first played in the Birmingham League in 1894. Its first success was winning the Birmingham League Championship in 1919. Its first ground was on land eventually taken over by the County High School for Girls in Junction Road, Stourbridge. It then moved to its present home in Amblecote on land which had been provided by the Earl of Stamford and Warrington of Enville Hall – who was also founder of Enville Cricket Club which still plays in the hall's grounds. On the left is Albert Dunham, who had a gent's outfitters in Stourbridge, early 1900s. On the right is James Dunham, possibly his son. Albert Dunham was a leading member of the Stourbridge town traders' team who used to play on Thursday afternoons (early closing day).

The former Amblecote Primary School in School Drive shortly before its demolition. For a time it was used as a civic hall for the tiny Amblecote Urban District Council and, later, as a temporary library before being declared structurally unsafe. Its demolition obviously coincided with the dawning of the age of conservation – note the piles of Staffordshire blue bricks being retained for use elsewhere.

High Street, Amblecote, close to the junction with Brettell Lane with the tram line junction clearly visible and a tramcar in the middle distance. Although some of the property on the left is still standing, the road today has been converted into a dual carriageway in an attempt to relieve traffic congestion.

The idea of using a captive balloon as a tourist attraction is not new as can be seen from this 1928 photograph of a balloon at the Corbett Hospital Fête. The same balloon was used for special events in the grounds of Dudley Castle. Seventy years later, history has repeated itself with a similar attraction being used in the castle grounds, which are now part of Dudley Zoo.

# ACKNOWLEDGEMENTS

The authors express their thanks to Hylma Douglas, Mrs B. Buffery, Mrs Walker, Miss Hewitt, Ken Rock, Alan Denham, Arthur Kimberley, John Edwards, John Haynes, David Hickman (Area Librarian), Gerald Milner and David Tooby for their generosity in the loan of photographs and volunteering a great deal of background information which would otherwise have gone unrecorded.

# BRITAIN IN OLD PHOTOGRAPHS

To order any of these titles please telephone our distributor, Littlehampton Book Services on 01903 721596
For a catalogue of these and our other titles please ring Regina Schinner on 01453 731114